I Love You, Mom

THUNDER BAY
P·R·E·S·S
SAN DIEGO

I *love* the **FUN** we have together!

I *love* the quiet times we share...

a *good* book,

a cup of *tea* and

my **MOM** sitting next to *me*.

A talk with you *always* makes it better...

A smile from you *always* makes it better...

A **HUG** with you *always* makes it better!

For **ALWAYS** cheering me on...

thank you, Mom.

For *helping* me learn,

for the stories and make-believe,

for bringing MAGIC to each day...

thank you, Mom.

Even when you make me want to

SHOUT...

I love you, Mom.

You *always* tell me I'm special…

You *always* ask how my day has been…

I can tell you anything, and you *always* listen.

In ALL ways you're *wonderful*, Mom.

I *love* spending time with you

no matter what we're doing.

You're the *best* cook I know,

the *best* mender of things,

the *best* finder,

creator and organizer

of EVERYTHING.

Mom, you're the *best*.

For letting me go out and *reach* for the STARS –

thank you, Mom!

Thank you for holding my hand

in THUNDERSTORMS.

I don't always get it right...

but you're ALWAYS there for *me*.

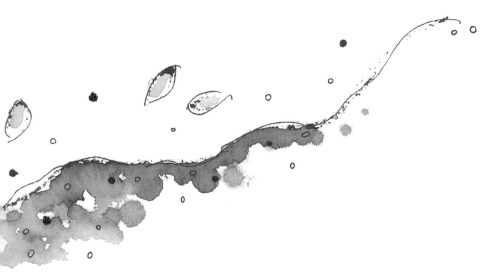

For getting home *late*,

for making a MESS,

for not always listening,

I'm *sorry*, Mom.

Thank you for telling me I *can* do ANYTHING.

I feel so *happy* when my phone rings

and I see it's YOU.

I *love* it when we sing along LOUDLY

to all our *favorite* songs!

When you're not close,

my **LOVELY** mom,

I miss you!

For EVERY...

"Remember your jacket!"

"Don't you worry!"

"Goodnight, sleep tight!"

"Good job, my darling!"

thank you, Mom.

I don't tell you often enough

how *beautiful* you are and how *loved* you are...

my AMAZING, *wonderful* mom!